I0485501

Creating Business Value

written by

Zsolt Szemerszky

Creating Business Value
- written by Zsolt Szemerszky -

First Printing: 2009

ISBN-13:   978-1519168368

ISBN-10:   1519168365

CreateSpace Independent Publishing Platform
Amazon.com

www.zsoltszemerszky.com

Dedication

"I dedicate this book to all the small business owners and entrepreneurs to ensure them a better understanding about the most basic principles in business."

Zsolt Szemerszky

Creating Business Value
- written by Zsolt Szemerszky -

Contents

Creating Business Value
- *written by Zsolt Szemerszky* -

Introduction

Zsolt Szemerszky is a National Quality Prize Winner Revenue Specialist and Author.

His aim to help people and corporations to achieve their highest ambitions.

Being an author of multiple books, published in over 50 countries world-wide helped Zsolt Szemerszky to create business values for people and to motivate them in the road towards their aims.

One of Zsolt's most quoted sentence is:

> *"Every mountain can be climbed*
> *just you have to find the appropriate way to it.*
> *If somebody does not achieve it's goal*
> *then he has not done everything to achieve it.*
> *The secret of success is persistence!"*

As one of the top business crisis advisor, revenue specialist, performance and marketing expert, Zsolt's books, videos, newsletters and appearances now inspire millions of people worldwide.

Creating Business Value
- written by Zsolt Szemerszky -

Creating Business Value

written by

Zsolt Szemerszky

Creating Business Value
- written by Zsolt Szemerszky -

Chapter 01
The angle of incidence of the Sun

One of the most basic and important business rule is that you are responsible for all your decisions, success or failures. Only you!

However hard it is you can not blame the external factors. We are in the same business jungle and the rules are the same for all of us. No exceptions. It is all upon you if you will survive or not. It is all upon you if you will be a Rabbit or you will become a Tiger. Now days the business is your jungle, your playground.

If you do not like to be a Rabbit then change it. You are the master of your destiny. Do not blame others, that's the game of losers and cowards.

Never blame outside factors, never say what could be if... You need to focus only on what you can do now with all your assets. You need to bring out the best as much as possible from your current, existing knowledge, assets.

Economy, politics, weather, your neighbor, etc... it is easy to blame these factors for your failure, but believe it or not these factors influence also your competition not only you.

You can not change these factors, just as you can not change the politics. You need to accept them, acknowledge the rules and go forward towards your aims. Sitting and waiting for the changes is equal with suicide because you will lose the control over things.

Chapter 02
Creating value in the business life of SMBs

The only enemy of a business is money. We are living in a terrible status of continuous effect, the media and marketing world revolves just around money, humanity has become dependent on money. However money is manipulated!

Through the work of banks and stock market also money has become a commodity and has become separated from the original value of the product or service, so this way money can be manipulated to gain profit. Money in itself has no value at all! Its value used to be determined by the product or service we get in return as an exchange for money.

Today the concept of money and the economy is fused. Unfortunately, the economic crisis is nothing more than the crisis of money, which is capable to pull with itself also the economy. We need to do two basic things in order to rise above the crisis: to create value and focus on the social capital, which means we need to take off our focus from the money!

The age of dinosaurs has expired and the world of marketing and sales approach is changing almost every year. The old methods are not effective and the focus is no longer on the product and the service itself, but on creating value and achieving trust. We need to dust off our old knowledge and develop new guidelines within our companies, businesses.

Our aim is to keep alive the continuously changing mind-set in the business ventures of our partners, as the company name initials indicates, our objective is no other than: Increasing Revenue and Business Optimization.

More than 10 years of market research has showed that there are basically five things that every business is strongly influenced by in its life, and which is not money!

1. Defining the target group

2. Creating value

3. Positioning

4. Appropriate marketing campaign

5. Utilizing social capital, networking

By applying adequately these points revenue growth is easily achieved so the revenue, cash flow increases as well. However, it is important to understand that when developing the above points the primary consideration is not money, but the corresponding value creation and correct communication towards our ideal target group.

Defining the target group

In addition to the entertainment electronics, marketing is the world's second fastest-growing business. It is especially interesting that 70% of people working in the marketing segment do not know what marketing is. It is almost a trend of today that everyone is competent in everything, so that specialization has disappeared. Marketing is not equal to the PR or sales tasks, functions.

Real marketing is not a simple advertisement. Real marketing is to catch the attention of your well-defined target group. If you just put advertisements into some magazines it is the same as hunting blindly. If you stay at the border of the forest where you want to hunt, and you shoot with eyes closed into the trees maybe you will hit an animal. But the chance you hit is very small...

The PR is not about press releases! It is the same case in marketing as it is in PR. If your promotion, campaign does not create, generate reactions then you throw your money out of the window.

RULE: The main task of the PR is to generate reaction!

Today the companies measure the PR values by Kilograms... The PR companies fill up 5-10 folders with press releases and advertisements... Who cares about the results? Who cares about the revenues? Only YOU!!!! When you have started a co-operation with a PR company you wanted more incoming money, not more costs for yourself... If we see the results from this point, from your owner point of view, then you can ask whether the 10 folders you received have given any results for you? No.

The number one task of marketing is defining the target group and the building of confidence. The target group is the minority who is interested in your offer and who interest you as well. Naturally you can have more target groups as well.

Trust is particularly important in the case of marketing, we call this credibility. This can help to measure, that if we say something how our target group will agree on it and receive it. Trust must be earned!

If you already have a target group who trusts you, you can gain a significant advantage during every marketing campaign.

But it is not enough to just define your target group, because without marketing you will loose your target group. This is the tricky part...

Marketing generates people who are interested in your product or solution. (And the sales people will close the deal.)

Creating value

Creating value in simple terms means creating products or services that people WANT!

Some years ago a huge new market has opened to us through the Internet. We overcame the invincible and were able to communicate our products to places which were unimaginable before. Distances disappeared and suddenly huge choices of products appeared.

It became increasingly easier to make business, particularly in the area of trade and by now anyone can start their own web shop in almost an hour. New opportunities have opened up for cheaters, and the previous confidence has turned over to mistrust. The new technologies unfortunately bring with themselves new abuses. Because of the daily scam letters or the time wasters, who want nothing more than to collect ideas, to benchmark, serious suspicions arose that has set back the intentions of the customers as well. Therefore, it is not enough if the product is just good.

Creating Business Value
- written by Zsolt Szemerszky -

The value has always been a relative concept, which is based on the personal judgement of the customer. The real product has never an absolute value, a product is worth as much as the buyer is willing to pay for it in exchange. All you need to achieve for this is for the customer to want the product.

The customer is capable to do only one thing, to bargain excellently. This is what the business life has taught the customer. If the same product is sold in more places, the customer will buy it where it is the cheapest. If you want to avoid that customers compare your prices, then show them that there are other considerations, criteria as well. This is what we call customer teaching. The aim is to show our customers that what they are buying is not a price tag, it is much more than that.

It is very important to remember that everyone can see the price of the product but not its value! We need to show and teach the value of the product in all cases.

The best is if we are able to add a plus to the product, which makes it unique, makes it more than its competitors and we offer them to those who have needs for exactly these pluses, who want exactly these products with their added values.

Anything can be sold to someone if he wants it even though he does not need it, but nothing can be sold that he does not want even if he needs it. The key is to find out what your client wants and to serve this need, since the value is no other than the fact of how much they want your product.

It is worth asking your customers what they want, what is most needed, what problems they face, then look at how your services, products help them and put the emphasis onto the problems, so that your customers see that they need this product, that they WANT it. If you do this well, then you have also almost positioned your product.

Positioning

The history of positioning goes back to the 1970s, it is possible to find a lot of ways since then how it has been used. But what does the word "positioning" mean? I try to demonstrate it to you with a few questions:

1., Who was the first man on the Moon?
Ok. Maybe it is easy, but who was the second? Do you know? No?! No problem, let's go forward...

2., Who was the first person who flew over the Atlantic Ocean?
Let me help you: Charles Lindbergh. And who was the second? Do you know? No?! No problem, let's go forward...

3., What is the highest mountain in the World?
Mount Everest. And the second one? Etc...

I hope you understand now the real meaning of positioning. People usually remember only the best, the first One. If you want to be successful in your PR, you have to place your product or solution to the first place in the mind of your target group.

If your product is not in the first place, you will loose a big potential market.

Never focus on the money, because the real power lies in the value, which is represented by your products or solutions. If you have learned to create value, then you still have further tasks since you need to sell your products or solutions.

If your PR is successful, then you have created value for your target group, that is you have well-positioned your product or solution. The next task for marketing is to look for your potential buyers, customers, who want your products, services. The sales performs the closing process, it makes it possible for your customers to buy from You.

The PR, marketing and sales functions should never be mixed up. Although one does not exist without the other, it is necessary to separate them and to know which is responsible for what, what is the end result we expect from each of them.

People want a product that has had a good PR, so it's easy to find out its potential circle of customers, the sales is just one simple step after this. Many companies, businesses commit an error that they only focus on the sales, while it carries out the least work within the work process. The actual work begins in the reverse way.

Appropriate marketing

Writing the right marketing text is one of the most difficult step during the marketing planning campaigns.

One of the most important thing when writing the marketing text is to try to describe the same thing as if we would be discussing it personally. If this is done then it just has to be combined and you are ready for the advertisement.

Creating Business Value
- written by Zsolt Szemerszky -

It is very important that we dare to write why the product or service is good for the target people, and what they need to do to make the products or services theirs. You should not be afraid to ask from the clients/customers or even to give instructions to them.

If your clients are contacted through the Internet or direct mail marketing campaign, the so-called Borden's formula can be a very useful thing. This comes from Richard C. Borden, head of New York University. He used this formula to originally make his classes more exciting, but it is perfect for attracting attention in offers, advertisements, letters.

The formula includes 4 simple steps:

1., "Who cares...."
Say something that will make the other look up, that will erase the other's indifference or carelessness and will make them immediately look up at you, will take you into consideration.

2., "Why am I talking about this"
Explain why it is important for the OTHER, why you want to talk or write to him or her. After this, tell your "story" very shortly, aiming to the point.

3., "For example...."
Tell the Other person one or more real life examples that illustrate and make your point more realistic.

4., "So what?"
Help the other Person get to the conclusion that you want him or her to get: why is it good, important for him or her, etc. if he or she does what you are asking him or her.

The Borden formula is a very efficient method, but you should never forget that writing marketing and advertisement texts is a separate profession. There are still lots of other tricks and methods, with which you can continuously develop your base of knowledge.

The only important thing in marketing campaigns, promotional materials and marketing texts is that they communicate. They should be personal and should communicate that they are a great opportunity for the person who is reading them and that they have been written exactly for him or her.

Utilizing social capital, networking

One of the greatest marketing method, which is undoubtedly the most effective marketing is the so-called recommendation or reference marketing.

Acquiring a new customer, client in all cases is a matter of trust. The customer who buys does it because he is confident that the product serves his interests and it makes his life easier, or it fulfills his desire. The point is that the purchase is always a matter of trust.

The high-quality products have in itself PR value, but it has to be made known to the outside world. The most effective marketing method for this is if we ask for so-called recommendations from our existing partners, clients. A product or service recommended by a client in all cases supports trust, however you should not forget that there are countless recommendations.

The goal is nothing more than to achieve, that our current customers offer our products, being consciously messengers of our business.

Creating Business Value
- written by Zsolt Szemerszky -

We must be conscious in the communications and we have to reach that our customers recommend our products, so that we can build a new communication line with the contact network of our clients.

The only effective method of this is if we build our marketing model in three dimensions. If we pay attention to our partners' needs and gain their trust, then the win-win-win business situation will be developed.

So it is easy to see that the root of the most successful reference marketing is the communication, conversation, continuous keeping in touch. It is important that it is no longer the product that matters but the man himself, his values. We will see that connection is equal to bond, which is equal to several more recommendations. If we pay attention to our partners, this process will be very much an automatic one and we will have a completely new "sales" team.

Its strength is unbelievable when a person recommends a product or service who understands us and whom we trust. 90% of these recommendations end with buying.

The world has changed radically over the years. In the past the world was in the hands of those who could offer a good product. Now-days the world is in the hands of those who have the right clients, customers, even if they have no products or services at all. The biggest value in business is the client, the customer.

In today's world the secret to successful business lies in the appropriate human relations, connections.

Chapter 03
Business Credit, Trust and Freedom

If you believe that your job is finished when your client or customer has bought a product or service from you, then you are wrong.

Your success is based on your satisfied and returning clients, customers!

If you were lucky enough to find a new customer, client then you need to keep him/her. You need to be sured that he/she is satisfied and he/she will recommend you.

With a satisfied customer you will have immediately two main advantages:

✓ You can capitalize his/her social network, since he/she will suggest your product to others

✓ You can ask for a kind and nice recommendation, which can strengthen your corporate image and credit.

To have a satisfied customer you need to keep the communication with him/her after the actual buying has been done. You need to check his/her impression about your products or solutions and you need to be sure that he/she can use your product or solution just as you can. If you show that you care about your customers, clients you can build up a relationship based on trust. And a trusted client will be always ready to endorse you, give you references or a simple defense for your credits against negative gossips, black PR or attacks on different forums.

Creating Business Value
- written by Zsolt Szemerszky -

You need to categorize your customers, clients:

1., possible customer

2., customer

3., satisfied and returning customer

Your aim should be to transform all your "possible customers" and "customers" into "satisfied and returning customers", because they will ensure your continuous success for the future.

Loyal and satisfied customers mean credit and trust in your market.

Chapter 04
You need to understand your market

Without understanding your business territory, your market you will maybe survive but you will never prosper. If your aim is generating revenue and profit you need to clearly understand what are the needs of your market, target group. You need to know what they are looking for, what is their decision criteria, etc...

There is a bad news for you...
There are different types of buyers:

some of them are only looking at the price

some of them are looking for the best quality

some of them are looking for the luxury or the prestige

some of them are looking for long term guarantees

some of them are looking for the added values

some of them simply make their decisions based on your personality

etc...

Many-many different needs but you need to know and handle them.

The price is only one factor and believe it or not, the price is not the most important one. If you will start to fight on the price, you will die.

You need to fight for your client! Whatever he or she wants...

Many companies have no other idea how to

communicate with their target group so they simply reduce the price. But this is just a silent and desperate scream for new customers, clients. If you understand the needs of your clients you do not need to reduce the price anymore. You will have the possibility to sell for a higher price than your competition without risking to loose your clients.

The most efficient way towards achieving business success is to understand the needs of your target group.

So how can you stabilize your market position?

If you had previous business experiences than hopefully you know by now that the marketing brings the revenue not the sales, not you product or solution.

Maybe you have a great product/solution but it remains just on the shelf. Does it bring you money? No.

If you do not use correctly marketing you will loose potential clients. Ok, you can say that the marketing is not about selling, the marketing is just marketing. No, you are wrong. The marketing is a weapon to sell well. If you look at the big companies, most of them do NOT use sales people, they use only marketing and the well-defined communication process.

Without marketing you will loose your target group.

Every CEO knows it, so they create the same mistake: they hire marketing managers...
You don't want to do the marketing because that is boring, you don't know it well, etc... If you would ask 10 CEOs, which area is the worst in their companies 9 will answer the marketing and PR.

So back to the first thought: you are hiring a marketing manager... Usually there is only one problem with them, they cost more than the money that they bring back to the company.

There are a lot of marketing experts but they are not looking for jobs. They do their own jobs.

There are only two solutions:

    you do the job or

    you will start to help somebody to learn the job.

No matter which solution you choose, you will need the KNOWLEDGE first!

You will not need books, not university programs, you will will need real daily experts, real knowledge from the business life.

One very important thing:
The marketing generates people who are interested in your product or solution. And the sales people will close the deal.

So you have a good need for good sales people.
You will need sales people who are with you not with your customers.

How can a sales person kill your business?
I tell you three examples:

1., Let's the client to push the price down. Usually the clients reaction to sales people is that a certain product or solution is cheaper in the next store, company, etc. The sales person usually say immediately, ok I give you 10% discount. But why??? At this point is the sales person working for you or working for the client???

2., A client or a possible buyer calls your company and the sales person in your company asks the possible buyer to write down his/her requests in an e-mail. NO! The 80% of the clients have no time to write e-mails, they need immediate answers, this is why they have called you directly.

3., If the sales can not manage the personal contacts.

You can create your own measuring system to control the sales work measuring system to control the sales work! This is what I like to do the most. :-)

A very simple example.
I had a big FMCG client. They had a lot of sales representatives.

The job was simple: the sales reps went to the stores and asked the orders. But the main task was to create a good relationship with the stores.

This company had in average 78 sales representatives in one country when I went there to help them. The CEO asked my help because the product was good but the revenue increased only 4-5% per year. It was not enough.

I created a little survey...
I asked some store owners about how their relationship with the sales representatives was, how they created the orders?

They said that the sales guys were there only in the first 3-4 times and after just called them for the new orders. Because the personal relations were not managed, cared for, looked after, the store owners never ordered anymore.

So I created a software solution to solve the problem.

Every sales representative had a Blackberry. Their job remained the same: to take the orders but the software wasn't the same...when the sales rep. put the order into the system, the software in the background checked the GPS coordinates. From this little measurement the company got the statistics that only 2.3 % of the orders were registered personally at the client through direct relationship. We showed this result to the sales people, and fired the worst 10. We told the sales rep. exactly what we are monitoring and that the company will be monitoring every sales order from now on.

Next month the registration done personally with the clients was 99.4% but the travel costs were still high.

I talked with the company CEO and we started to register the routes as well and analyze them...

After the second month the fuel costs decreased by 72%, because the sales people went to the client in the optimal route and the orders from the personal visitings were still 99.4%!!!

We saved costs on fuel and won more orders because of the personal contacts.

That's simple. Measure your marketing and sales and never trust in your employees. This is business!

Chapter 05
Using Formulas in the business life

If your clients are contacted through the Internet or direct mail marketing campaign, the so-called Borden's formula can be a very useful thing. This comes from Richard C. Borden, head of New York University. He used this formula to originally make his classes more exciting, but it is perfect for attracting attention in offers, advertisements, letters.

The Borden formula

The formula includes 4 simple steps:

1., "Who cares...."
Say something that will make the other look up, that will erase the other's indifference or carelessness and will make them immediately look up at you, will take you into consideration.

2., "Why am I talking about this"
 Explain why it is important for the OTHER, why you want to talk or write to him or her. After this, tell your "story" very shortly, aiming to the point.

3., "For example...."
Tell the Other person one or more real life examples that illustrate and make your point more realistic.

4., "So what?"
Help the other Person get to the   conclusion that you want him or her to get: why is it good, important for him or her, etc. if he or she does what you are asking him or her.

The Borden formula is a very efficient method, but you should never forget that writing marketing and advertisement texts is a separate profession. There are still lots of other tricks and methods, with which you can continuously develop your base of knowledge.

The only important thing in marketing campaigns, promotional materials and marketing texts is that they communicate. They should be personal and should communicate that they are a great opportunity for the person who is reading them and that they have been written exactly for him or her.

AIDA Formula

Attention - Interest - Desire - Action

Attention
Say something that will attract your reader's attention

Interest
Tell the other person why he or she should be interested in the issue and why he or she should believe what you are saying.Prove that what you are saying is true and real (case studies, offerings, opinions, references, etc.)

Desire
Write down, list your product's or services' advantages, effects on the other person's life, business etc. You should achieve that the other person should WANT, desire your Product, service or You as a professional, what you are offering.

Action
Tell the other person to react to your offer if the interest has been lighten up and tell him or her to do it now.

Best practices for Offer writing

Desire - Problem - Fears - Solution - Advantages - References

Desire:
Write down what you want to sell

Problem:
Describe why it would be necessary for the other person to buy it, to take what you are offering.

Fears:
You need to list here the excuses that clients might say

Solution:
Repeat in 2-3 lines the solution. You mention the price here!

Advantages:
What is the advantage by buying your product or service

References:
Client or reference opinion, reference

CV formula

Desire - Problem - Fears - Solution - Advantages - References

Desire:
I want to have a position as a project manager in your company.

Problem: This would be good for you because...with my experiences....I can add to your success in this way.....

Fears: Many companies do not take, consider applicants over 40 years old. They forget that between 20 and 30 years old people change their jobs more often, while a person more mature is much more loyal to their jobs, positions and consider their tasks, jobs as part of their whole life.

Solution:
The expertise and experience is priceless.

Advantage:
I am not a simple expert, professional, your company forms part of my Life...

References:
Reference from who you know, who knows you as well.

Chapter 06
Where is the money magnet?

Let's start with a simple issue.

How can you increase your revenue?
IT is easy, forget waste...

Every Euro or Dollar that you payed for marketing, pr, press release, advertise, etc.. which never generated the necessary revenue is a waste. Time, money and energy. What did you do really? You missed the chance to win new partners and sell products...

What we know: The aim of the marketing is to sell. Sell solutions/products and increase your revenue. That's it.

Two typical mistakes that sales people do:

1., Don't know the target group

2., Start immediately with an offer

If you want to be efficient, you can define your target.
If you create a good marketing campaign that you like, your secretary likes and your family likes, who cares?... They ARE NOT your target group. You have to focus on your target group, because they will buy your solutions/products and they will give you the money. If you want gratulations from your friends and family, collecting votes, go to be a politician. Politics is all about votes.

The amateurs are trying to sell products to everybody, but the professionals select the target. Later I will tell you how.

Creating Business Value
- written by Zsolt Szemerszky -

If you know your target exactly, then you can communicate to her/him directly, personalized.

If you think that you sell bread and everybody needs bread, YOU ARE WRONG! A lot of people has bread cooking machine at home. They are not your target.

A small example: In Toronto there is a tatoo saloon. In the window you can see the following text: "What are you looking? If you want a tatoo come in, other case go to hell..."

Yes, this is aggressive, maybe... I imagine that the old couples walk around and they see this slogan in the window: It 's awful... For them yes, but they are the real target for a Tatoo?? No, I do not think so. The saloon found the target, they created the perfect style and they are full with teenagers, who want tatoo. It was an excellent marketing strategy.

If you know your target, do you thing the price is important? No!!! Never!

My question: Remember, when you bought your last car, did you buy the cheapest one? Did you say to the dealer that you need the cheapest one, no matter what the colors and options no are? I do not think so... Why? Because everybody is different and everybody has own feelings, subjective decisions. Just like you!

Please never fall in love of your products or your advertisements, your main aim is the result that they give you.

I know 63 types of marketing. The people who finish the university they know around 3... But one thing is common in everybody: we always forget why we are creating marketing campaigns...

Never forget:

marketing = helps to sell

sales = brings revenue and money

You should memorize now the right steps:

1., Solution/Product

2., Define the target group

3., Creating marketing campaign

4., Knowing the reaction of your target, know what they really want

5., Offer

6., Sell

7., After sales

If you miss one of these steps you will lose 70% potential money. Believe me.

I have a friend who has an event management company in Europe. They are creating luxury events for the high end people. His problem is, how can you reach your ideal target?

They made the biggest mistake ever! They gave the whole marketing to a big marketing and communication company for fix monthly payment.
RULE: Never trust a company who is working for fixed money. If they work for fix they are not motivated and 99% they just want your money.

So this marketing company created a lot of media campaign for 75.000 Euros. The result was 2 types of flyers, 10 advertisements and only 1 buyer. The whole job lasted for 3 months. 3 months for only one buyer who just payed 15.000 Euro. The event management company just wasted the time. They missed the chance to win new partners and sell products because of the wrong strategy they chose. In this case they spent around 75.000 Euro easily without any result.

Before you start a marketing campaign first define your target.

The real marketing is to catch the attention of your well defined target group. If you just put advertisements into some magazines it is the same as hunting blind. If you stay in the border of the forest, you close your eyes and just shoot into the trees maybe you will hit an animal. But the chance you hit is very small...

Never forget:

    marketing = helps to sell

    sales = brings revenue and money

So this guy payed for big media advertisements, merchandize materials, and for some press articles. When we talked he said he is disappointed in the people because nobody wants to buy. He said everybody is afraid of economy crash.
I said to him this is bullshit. So we started to work a little together. I said to him work with me for two days and we will find 10 ways how can you communicate to your target group without paying for marketing...

So what can we do in this situation with minimal budget?

Advertising? NO! I said minimal budget!!! You can pay for any advertisement but you will not communicate to you target group.

Let's find the target group, the real target group.
The background of the company: luxury travels, European car tours, race track days, etc...

We defined the target group and we started to work. I share you two ideas from the ten what we created:

They focused on everyone who read Playboy, Financial Times, Vogue, etc... They used the blind hunting in the forest strategy...

We picked each programs separately and defined the best target group for them.

ADVICE 01:

So first we picked the exclusive travel program.

The target group was the wealthy people.

The main aim: find potential partners, create a big marketing e-mail list for the future promotions

Facts: everybody likes traveling but nobody wants to spend a lot of money for an exclusive travel.

From 2003-2008 I worked with IBM and we used a "You pass, we pay" program. The main point was that if you start a course and after you pass in the exam you get back your money. So this was our starting point.

So we created the "You travel and we pay" program.

What we needed first were the personal contacts. We do not want to waste our time for cold calls. If somebody calls you from the street to sell you something usually you do not listen to her/him. But if somebody calls you, that your friend gave her/him your contact then you will listen to the offer. Why? Because your friend offered and you trust in your friend.

So the campaign was the following. Register to our travel and propose us people. If somebody registers from the people you have proposed we pay back to you 15% from your travel price.

The result was amazing. The people wanted to came for free so within 2 weeks we had an over 5.000 names marketing list with the requested target group.

Yes we gave 15% discount after every new person but the margin was bigger because of the lot more registered people. Remember: The people want to get things for cheap or free...

ADVICE 02:

After we chose the European car tours program.

They focused until now on rich and wealthy young guys. Yes they were right, but...

I started to focus on another target group the new car owners.

What we did was we started to create connections directly with a lot of luxury car stores in Europe. We contacted them first via e-mail, just checked the reactions.

This was not a cost and after if they were open, they could call them with Skype for example.

The only investment was 4-5 hours research and 2-3 hours Skype phone calls. That's it.

The possible revenue was around 70% higher than any kind of advertisement! Why? What's the offer?

Everybody who buys a new luxury car wants to try it and show everybody that he has a Ferrari/ Lamborghini/Porsche/etc...

After we agreed with the dealer, they gave a bonus or gift for the customers.

Gift: Because the customer bought the car, he got a possibility to a luxury car travel in a better price. He payed the standard price and the passengers were free. He won, and they also won!

The only thing what was important that they motivated the dealer as well, because the dealer brought them the opportunity.

The dealer won a possibility to be an official sponsor or got a free travel, etc... The travelers were potential luxury car buyers and when they know the dealer's name maybe the dealer will have a good business later.

This is a long term investment for the dealer which brings media attention, marketing, public press and potentially new clients. BUT!!! The most important it does not cost any money for the dealer! WIN-WIN situation! Marketing without money investment in the whole Europe.

Creating Business Value
- *written by Zsolt Szemerszky* -

CONCLUSION:

These two advices do not cost money only time. Around one day each.

I had a lot of other practical examples and ideas but I can not share my best ones here in Facebook.

The most of the marketing and PR agencies want money for advertising and media (TV, press, online) campaigns. These campaigns are very beautiful and powerful, but never reach the maximum potential. But the marketing company never cares because they created and they got the money... It is usually bad only for the client.

The only way when the marketing is good if it gives more...

The worst that you can do if you push yourself and then usually the answer is: "OK, I am thinking, maybe I will buy it... But there are a lot of other products..." Result: 15-30% of buyers, maximum

The hardest thing if you communicate that you need money. This never works. The best way if you can show to your possible customer that you want to help him, you want the best for him. Never give an offer first!!!

If you do something and you believe in your product you can not be cheap. Remember the people DO NOT WANT CHEAP things. The cheapest wins is a bullshit, it is just a legend, it is just for amateur marketing companies. Remember your car buying... You bought the cheapest? NO! In this generations sometimes the cheap things are sticky... If you are more than half cheaper than the others that case you can communicate well: WHY??

- 41 -

If you just communicate: Because we are better. Who cares? A small example.

You are going to the sport store because you want a new ball. There are pink balls for 5 Euro and blue balls for 7 Euro. The pink is cheaper but you hate pink. The sales guy tell you that these balls are the same quality maybe the pink is better, all made in China, but blue is a unique color, but everybody buys pink. You will be everybody or you will pay a little bit more for the color that you want?

If the product is good and your marketing communicates absolutely to the target group, your customers are ready to pay more, believe me. This is very important, sales is not price fight, NEVER!

What I really wanted to show you that sometimes you pay more than necessary for marketing, maybe without results.

What you should memorize in this time the right steps:

1., Solution/Product

2., Define the target group

3., Creating marketing campaign

4., Knowing the reaction of your target, know what they really want

5., Offer

6., Sell

7., After sales

The marketing is full with opportunities.

Chapter 07
Lists

One of the biggest value in a company is its clients, partners.

A well structured company needs at least two different types of lists:

1., List of the existing clients

2., List of the potential clients, customers

With these lists you can reach potential customers, and you can generate income in various economic situations. The most important is that you need to have a daily list of your clients and a four-five times bigger list of your possible, potential customers. This is database marketing (with existing clients and potential customers).

With a proper database marketing list you can easily reduce your marketing costs. Just think about how much does it cost to reach 10.000 people with a newspaper advertisement? Now compare it with a simple e-mail campaign. Millions versus zero.

However many companies make the same mistake when they push immediately their offers onto their possible clients, customers. With this kind of aggressive steps you just scare off all possible clients, customers and you will eventually lose them.

The most important factor in the database marketing is to build up your trust. Give them weekly or monthly advices, practices, education and useful information. You need to reach their attention and later you can easily catch their interest. When the time comes and they would like to buy a product like yours, they will remember you and you will have a huge business advantage because of your already built up trust.

Of course later you can offer special promotions or products but never in the initial rounds. If you have well secured your trust with your potential clients, customers they will be 70% more open to accept your special offer. With this you can create promotions and you can generate incomes in any business or economic situation.

Chapter 08
Two way communication

In life one of the most important thing is communication. Communication should be two ways every time.

If you do not answer you not do respect me. That's simple. Or my campaign is bad and it does not communicate well... Let's look at this a little in details.

Most of the company leaders are afraid from the PR and marketing areas because they have had bad experiences. In the last 10 years most of the companies just bought advertisements and never generated big results. A little example: I consulted a company last year and the CEO spent lots of money for campaigns.

I asked him, the company CEO, what the result was? He said some generation of new sales.

I asked him whether he was satisfied? He said no...

I asked him what he thought the problem was? He said the problem might be with the product because the PR company made a lot of beautiful advertisements and they presented 7 folders full with press releases.

I pointed to him that this was the problem...

The PR is not about press releases! This is the same case in marketing just as it is in PR.

If your promotion, campaign does not create, generate reactions then you throw your money out of the window. RULE: The main task of the PR is to generate reaction! Not articles, press releases, REACTION!

Creating Business Value
- written by Zsolt Szemerszky -

Today the companies measure the PR values by Kilograms... The PR companies fills up 5-10 folders with press releases and advertisements... Who cares about the results? Who cares about the revenues? Only YOU!!!! When you started the co-operation with the PR company you wanted more incoming money, not more costs for yourself... If we see the result from this point, from your owner point of view, then you can ask whether the 10 folders give you any result? No.

We use the communication verbal or written, because we want reactions. If there were no reactions then it was just a wasted time. The main task of the communication is to send a message to people and to get back a reaction or an answer.

Most of the marketing companies always break this rule. I always see campaigns like this: "Buy Lemonde!" Ok, thanks maybe next time. Never tell me as a client what I really want...

As I said before: Never trust in a company who is working just for fix amounts. Never. If they work for fix amounts they are not motivated and 99% of times they just want your money. If you can create (maybe with a good help) a two way communication channel with your clients, possible buyers you will be much more efficient!

One more rule in PR: PR means that you have to make known a product/solution in a wider group, and you have to create a good opinion about that product/ solution.

You can not sell if people do not know your product or if they have a bad opinion about your product. How many sales people can sell a very bad quality, unnamed product? Not so many...

You can maybe say that people did not want to buy your product/solution... But No, I think you did not find the best offer for them. People are always ready to buy! The only mistake you made was that your PR was not good, in all other cases you can make revenue easily.

If you or your consultant partner can create a good opinion about your product/solution and can make it known in wider areas, then you can sell in a much easier way.

Chapter 09
How can you earn money ASAP!?!

There are often lots of situations in business life when you need money ASAP. Maybe it is not necessary but, you want a new car, you want to travel somewhere or you just do not want to ask a loan for your new investment.

So, do you want to earn some money ASAP? I teach you a good way, how you can achieve it.

I have a very useful strategy, my friend Robert used this since 10 years, we used this with many companies when consulting with them.

Step ONE:
Choose your best and most successful product/solution which is available immediately in your stock.

Step TWO:
Remember when and how you sold most of your product/solution.

Step THREE:
How can you reach your possible target group and in what kind of communication ways?

Step FOUR:
What can you add to your product/solution that increases more buying?

Step FIVE:
Test the possible options!

Step SIX:
Advertise a fast promotion.

Step SEVEN:
Ask your target group, why didn't they buy your product/solution?

Step EIGHT:
Solve the problems.

Step NINE:
Repeat your campaign.

Important, if you want to earn money, always use ready made products/solutions. If the product was good in the last years that case you can use it easily for earn money now.

Chapter 10
Roulette

If you are a successful entrepreneur or company owner pay attention not to put all the incomes back into your company. Otherwise it is like playing in the casino and putting your money all the time on the Red. It is committing suicide against yourself.

There are a lot of small companies who have no reserves. Things happen, economics and politics always change so you need to have a reserve to survive. Usually the reserve equals around eight or twelve months of your operating costs.

The income of your company is very similar to your private investment portfolio. You can not put everything into the Trade market you need to diversify your portfolio. Without diversification you act like a Kamikaze.

Lets say you need to create at least three different accounts:
1., Daily operation account

2., Future developments account

3., Security reserve

The best and most effective way if you create a company rule similar as this:

60% of the incomes go directly to the Daily operation account

30% of the incomes go directly to the Future developments account

10% of the incomes go directly to the Security reserve account

The most important thing is that you need to plan your business model based on the incomes of the Daily operation account and not on the total incomes of your company.

Liability disclaimer

This book/e-book is not a substitute for independent professionals, investment or legal advice. Present book serves as the writer's interpretation of his personal business views, without specific advice on any personal or corporate requirements. Use of any information from this book or any other book or web site referred to is for general information only and does not represent advice either expressed or implied. You are encouraged to seek professional, legal or investment advice.

Accordingly, the author, his publishers and affiliates disclaim that the information provided should not be treated as advice. Furthermore, it is a strict condition of the that any individual reading the book recognizes and accepts unreservedly that all information, analyses, projections, forecasts, expectations, or outcomes relating to past, present, or future financial markets performance, economic activity, or investment or trading instruments, are provided exclusively for academic purposes and that such information must not in any way be construed as general or personal advice to invest or trade in any financial market or security.

The author or publishers shall not be held liable for any losses incurred by anyone who follows or acts on the opinions, views, or forecasts expressed in any form in this e-book, on any other websites or from individuals connected by hyperlink to or from this website. Anyone reading this book is solely responsible for their interpretation of its contents and for their own decisions and actions. The foregoing applies also to correspondence (including private emails), to posts on other websites (including internet message boards and public discussion forums), and to articles published in other mass media.

You should make your own enquiries before entering into any business decision on the basis of the information or material on this e-book. Please ensure you contact an adviser directly to discuss your particular circumstances and how the information provided applies to your situation. Past performance is not indicative of future performance, and involves substantial risks. All readers should consult their own Authorized Business Adviser and/or, Solicitor or other specialists before placing money at risk or attempting to implement any of the strategies discussed, and should always employ prudent policies and practices appropriate to their own particular circumstances.